To my gorgeous and wonderful friend Penny. Have a fabulous Christmas 2022, lots of love from Jules xxx

RED SAILS & PILCHARDS

CORNISH HARBOURS IN THE AGE OF SAIL

Written & Illustrated by Matt Johnson

Published by Design For Today, 2022 • Printed at Graphius NV, Ghent on 120gsm Munken Pure Rough
Design For Today, 30 Victoria Road, Topsham, Devon, EX3 0EU
designfortoday.co.uk

ISBN 978-1-912066-93-3

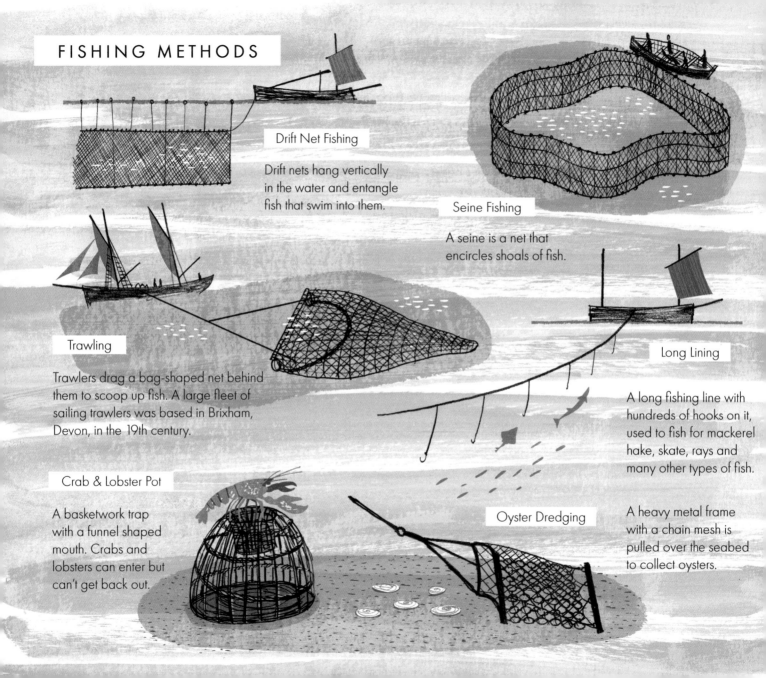

FISHING METHODS

Drift Net Fishing

Drift nets hang vertically in the water and entangle fish that swim into them.

Seine Fishing

A seine is a net that encircles shoals of fish.

Trawling

Trawlers drag a bag-shaped net behind them to scoop up fish. A large fleet of sailing trawlers was based in Brixham, Devon, in the 19th century.

Long Lining

A long fishing line with hundreds of hooks on it, used to fish for mackerel hake, skate, rays and many other types of fish.

Crab & Lobster Pot

A basketwork trap with a funnel shaped mouth. Crabs and lobsters can enter but can't get back out.

Oyster Dredging

A heavy metal frame with a chain mesh is pulled over the seabed to collect oysters.

A fish auction on the beach

Fishing has been a way of life in Cornwall for thousands of years and helped shape its unique identity. This book celebrates the ingenuity of the Cornish fishing communities in the 19th and early 20th century, when the industry was at its peak. It is an introduction to the techniques that were developed and the beautiful boats, harbours and artefacts that were crafted in the era of sail, before the arrival of the larger motor-powered trawlers, and the decline of local fisheries.

Pyskessa re beu fordh vewa yn Kernow dres milyow a vledhynnyow ha re weresas ow furvya hy honanieth unnik. An lyver ma a solempen ynjynieth kemenethow pyskessa Kernow y'n 19ves hag a-varr y'n 20ves kansbledhynnyow, pan o an diwysyans orth y ughella pryck. Komendyans yw dhe'n teknegow a veu displegys ha dhe'n kokow teg, porthow ha taklennow a veu gwrys y'n oos a wolyow, kyns devedhyans a vrassa kokow-draylya nerthys gans jynnow, ha difyk an pyskegi leel.

FISHING AND THE CORNISH LANGUAGE

Many Cornish words were preserved in the dialect of fishermen and collected by Cornish language revivalists, such as Robert Morton Nance. Some Cornish and dialect words are included throughout in *italics*.

This is Mevagissey Harbour in the very early 20th century. Fishing was still the village's main industry and hundreds of its men and boys worked on the boats. Many more people, including women and children, worked in related jobs, such as curing fish and making boats, sails, nets, baskets, barrels, and rope.

The harbour was crammed with luggers: locally-built, with black-tarred hulls and reddish-brown sails. Powered by the wind and oars, they fished for pilchards, herring, mackerel and other species plentiful around the Cornish coast.

ST IVES

QUAY STREET

Railways came to Cornwall in the second half of the 19th century, allowing fish to be sent for sale upcountry.

Harbours were also used to ship minerals from the mines and quarries. At Newquay, a railway line was built directly into the harbour.

NEWQUAY

Stone piers, like Smeaton's Pier in St Ives, were built in harbours all around Cornwall to protect the fishing fleets from rough seas.

ISLES OF SCILLY

Round Island

Sevenstones Lightship

SEVENSTONES

Hugh Town

St Agnes

Wolf Rock

Bishop Rock

Newlyn has been Cornwall's major fishing port since the 19th century.

Pendeen Watch

Longships

Priest's Cove

Sennen

Porthgwarra

St Ives

Godrevy

Portreath

Porthtow

St

Hayle

Camborne

Redruth

Penzance

Newlyn

Marazion

Mousehole

Penberth

Lamorna

NEWLYN

Porthleven

Helston

Gweek

Port Na

Helford

Porthal

Mullion

Porthous

Covera

Cadgwith

Lizard Point

FISHING VILLAGES & PORTS

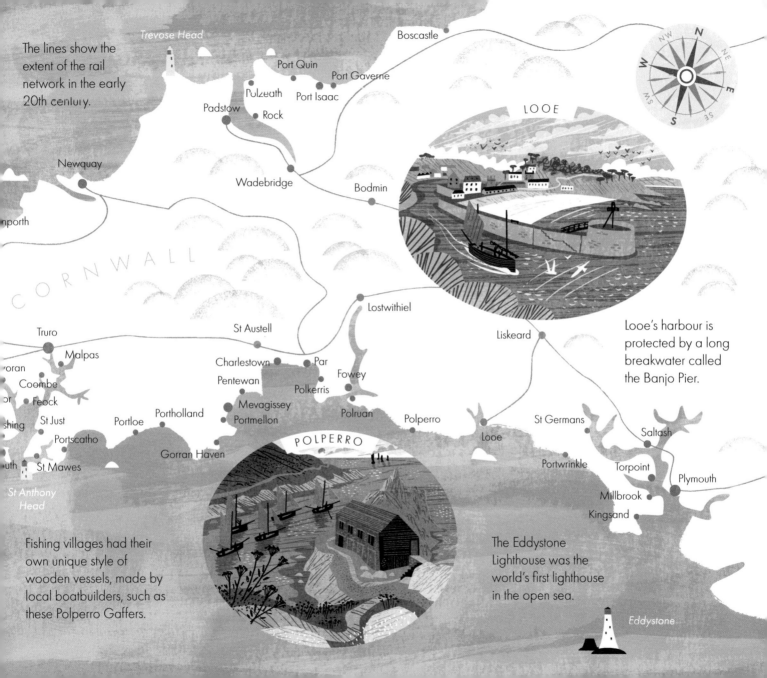

The lines show the extent of the rail network in the early 20th century.

Trevose Head

Boscastle

Port Quin
Port Gaverne
Pulzeath
Port Isaac
Padstow
Rock

Newquay

...nport

Wadebridge

Bodmin

LOOE

CORNWALL

Lostwithiel

Liskeard

Looe's harbour is protected by a long breakwater called the Banjo Pier.

Truro
Malpas
...oran
Coombe
...r
Feock
...shing
St Just
Portscatho
...uth
St Mawes

St Anthony
Head

St Austell

Charlestown
Pentewan

Portholland
Portloe
Mevagissey
Portmellon
Gorran Haven

Par
Fowey
Polkerris

Polruan

Polperro

St Germans
Saltash
Torpoint
Plymouth
Portwrinkle
Millbrook
Kingsand

Looe

POLPERRO

Fishing villages had their own unique style of wooden vessels, made by local boatbuilders, such as these Polperro Gaffers.

The Eddystone Lighthouse was the world's first lighthouse in the open sea.

Eddystone

Sprat / *Herring-Bairn*

Herring / *Hernen Wyn*

Mackerel / *Brithel, Bre'al*

Bream / *Dama Goth*

John Dory

Pilchard / *Hernen*

Sea Bass

Plaice / *Lith*

Monk Fish / *Mulvainah*

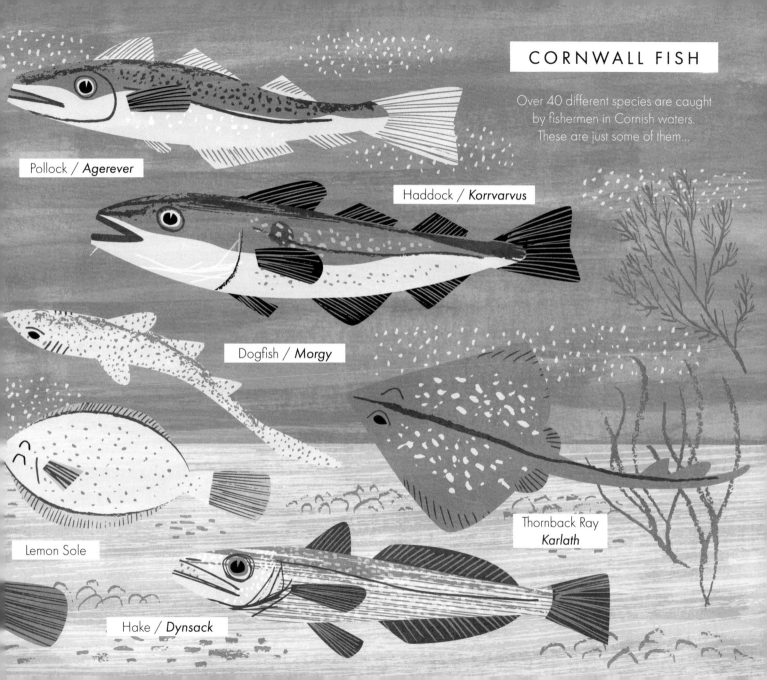

CORNWALL FISH

Over 40 different species are caught
by fishermen in Cornish waters.
These are just some of them...

Pollock / **Agerever**

Haddock / **Korrvarvus**

Dogfish / **Morgy**

Lemon Sole

Thornback Ray
Karlath

Hake / **Dynsack**

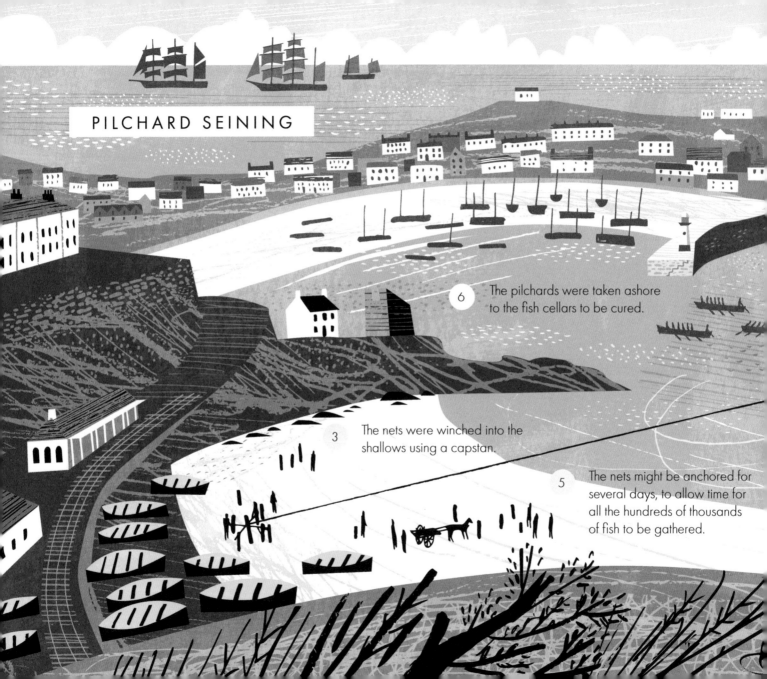

PILCHARD SEINING

6   The pilchards were taken ashore to the fish cellars to be cured.

3   The nets were winched into the shallows using a capstan.

5   The nets might be anchored for several days, to allow time for all the hundreds of thousands of fish to be gathered.

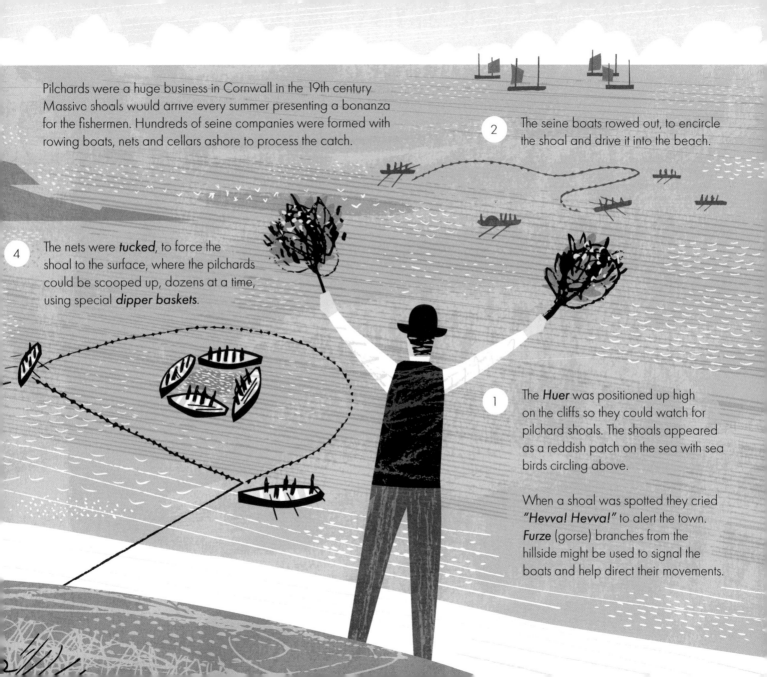

Pilchards were a huge business in Cornwall in the 19th century. Massive shoals would arrive every summer presenting a bonanza for the fishermen. Hundreds of seine companies were formed with rowing boats, nets and cellars ashore to process the catch.

2 The seine boats rowed out, to encircle the shoal and drive it into the beach.

4 The nets were *tucked*, to force the shoal to the surface, where the pilchards could be scooped up, dozens at a time, using special *dipper baskets*.

1 The *Huer* was positioned up high on the cliffs so they could watch for pilchard shoals. The shoals appeared as a reddish patch on the sea with sea birds circling above.

When a shoal was spotted they cried *"Hevva! Hevva!"* to alert the town. *Furze* (gorse) branches from the hillside might be used to signal the boats and help direct their movements.

CURING PILCHARDS

Once ashore the pilchards were gutted, salted and packed into casks. The casks were pressed to extract oil, which was used for lighting lamps as well as in tanning and paint. A huge number of the casks were sold to Catholic countries, where the pilchards were eaten during Lent, when meat was forbidden. In the early 19th century, Cornish pilchards were also sold to British sugar plantation owners, to feed their enslaved workers in the Caribbean, a significant but lesser known trade.

By the mid-nineteenth century the pilchard shoals began to dwindle in size and soon disappeared completely. The seine industry collapsed and Cornish fisherman had to venture further out to sea for their catches.

DRIFTING

As the seine industry declined, more fishermen took up drifting with luggers. Drift fishing was more flexible as they could sail to wherever the fishing was best. The boats and nets cost a fraction of the price of those used for seining, putting them in reach of individual fishermen.

Their main fishing grounds were south of the Eddystone and west of the Isles of Scilly. In the summer they also fished for herring in the Irish and North Seas. Like the Devon trawlers, the drifters were blamed for breaking up the pilchard shoals and were forbidden from using nets within three miles of the shore during the pilchard season.

1

Before going to sea, fishermen had to decide if it was safe. There were no weather forecasts and they had to rely on their own experience and intuition. Some ports had a barometer in a glass case on the quay, to help warn of bad weather.

2

Once they reached the fishing grounds, local knowledge and observations were used to locate the fish, like the colour of the water or diving gannets.

3

The nets were set before sunset. *Towl ros* means "cast net" in Cornish

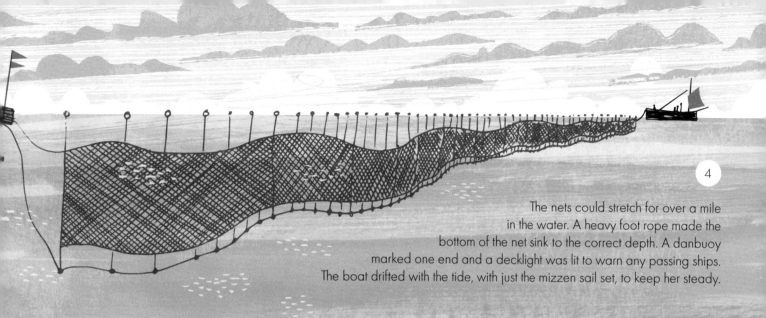

4

The nets could stretch for over a mile
in the water. A heavy foot rope made the
bottom of the net sink to the correct depth. A danbuoy
marked one end and a decklight was lit to warn any passing ships.
The boat drifted with the tide, with just the mizzen sail set, to keep her steady.

5

The fishermen then had a few hours' wait. At least one
man would need to keep watch, while the others rested
or fished with hand lines to pass the time. Meanwhile,
with any luck, plenty of fish would swim into the nets
and get caught.

The nets were hauled in after midnight. Some boats had a steam powered capstan to help with the heavy ropes, but it was still a long, hard task. The ropes and nets would be cold and heavy with seawater, and the work would take several hours. The youngest member of the crew would go below and coil the ropes.

The nets themselves were pulled on board by hand and the fish shaken out and sorted, counted and put in the fish berth. Some boats had a chute in the deck called a *scudding hole*, that allowed the fish to be swept straight down into the hold. If a few of the fish were bitten in half, they'd know a seal had made a meal of their catch.

If the catch was poor, then the men would spend another night fishing and another, until they had enough. A ton of ice might be taken to sea in larger boats to keep the fish fresh. Once the fish berth was full, it was a race to port, as the first boats back got the highest price. Reaching port in time meant the fish could be sent upcountry by sea or rail.

Otherwise, they might be sold locally by *Jousters* for a lower price. Cornish families would buy a thousand or more pilchards and salt them in pots called *bussas*, to make sure they had enough food through the winter.

"Meat, money and light - all in one night."
Cornish saying

The mackerel driver was a large lugger used for fishing mackerel and herring with drift nets. They were fast, seaworthy boats that could venture hundreds of miles out to sea or up the coast in search of shoals.

Topsail

Foresail

Mizzen Mast

Mizzen

Jump Stay

Reef Lines

Fore Mast

Forkel
with Lamp

Shroud

Tiller

Steam Capstan

Cavel

Hatches

Companion
Way

Stern

Scud Hook

Scottle

Fish Berth

Net Room
or Sheet

Rudder

Bow

Gear

Net
Foot Rope

Shifting Ballast

Ballast

Stove & Boiler

Forefoot

Keel

MACKEREL DRIVER
1900

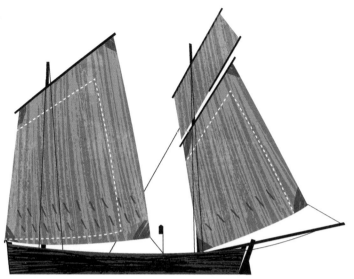

The pilchard driver was a smaller drifter of 30-40 feet in length.

A St Ives mackerel driver with topsail and big mizzen known as a **burning heart**. Smaller sails called *jiggers* were set in stronger winds.

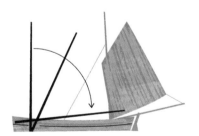

A slot called the **scottle** allowed the foremast to be lowered while the boat was fishing.

After 1910 fishing boats began to have engines and propellers installed. Wheelhouses were also added, to give some shelter on deck.

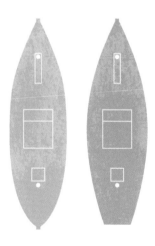

Luggers in West Cornwall often had pointed sterns, to fit more boats in their cramped harbours and cope with swells, whereas boats from further east had square transoms.

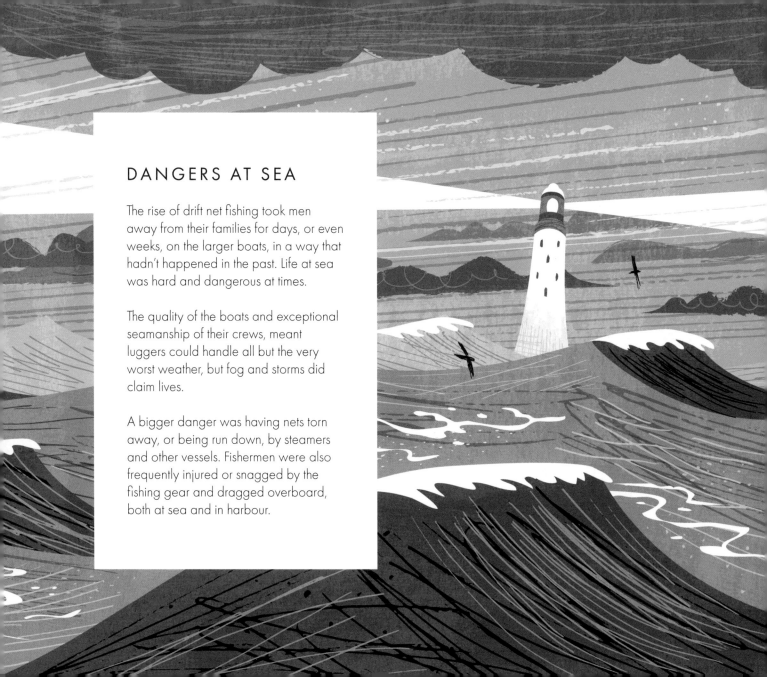

DANGERS AT SEA

The rise of drift net fishing took men away from their families for days, or even weeks, on the larger boats, in a way that hadn't happened in the past. Life at sea was hard and dangerous at times.

The quality of the boats and exceptional seamanship of their crews, meant luggers could handle all but the very worst weather, but fog and storms did claim lives.

A bigger danger was having nets torn away, or being run down, by steamers and other vessels. Fishermen were also frequently injured or snagged by the fishing gear and dragged overboard, both at sea and in harbour.

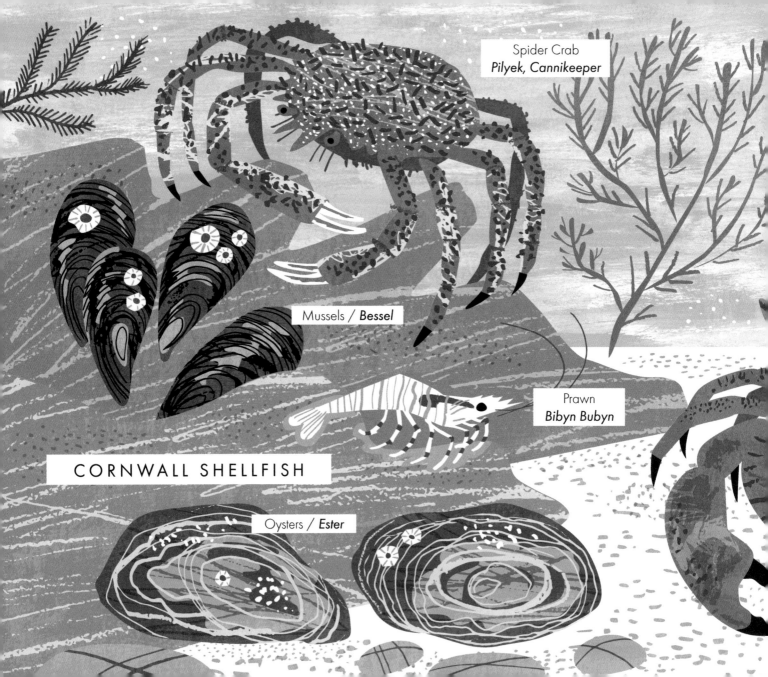

Spider Crab
Pilyek, Cannikeeper

Mussels / *Bessel*

Prawn
Bibyn Bubyn

CORNWALL SHELLFISH

Oysters / *Ester*

Velvet Swimming Crab

Crawfish / **Gaver Vor**

Lobster / **Legest**

rown Crab
Kanker

Scallop
Krogen Sen Jamys

WITHY POTS

Basketwork "inkwell" pots were used in Cornwall to catch crabs, crawfish and lobsters. Willow was grown in withy gardens specially for this purpose. Withies were cut and stuck in a *crabbut-stand* to start a new pot. A skilled maker could complete a withy pot in a few hours.

Bait on
wooden
skiver
sticks

Mouth

Stone weights

Smaller boats with a crew of just one or two were used to set pots.
They would be set in strings of up to 30 pots on a single rope. Cork buoys
on each end would mark their position and they would be hauled up once
or twice a day. A withy pot might give a year's service before it rotted,
but if a fisherman was unlucky and a storm hit,
they might lose all their pots in one night.

OYSTER DREDGING

Oysters were dredged in Cornish estuaries, like the River Fal, using gaff-rigged working boats or oar-powered punts.

The punt was anchored and the anchor line winched in, dragging the dredge along the river bed. The dredge was then hauled up over the stern and its contents emptied onto the *culch board* to be sorted.

OYSTER PUNT

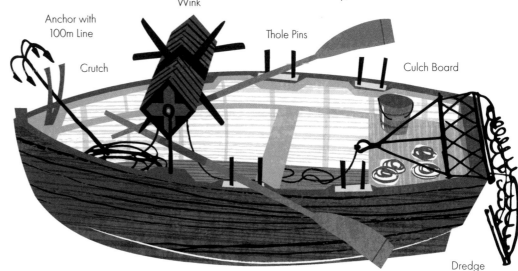

Motorised dredging is banned on the River Fal, so oysters are still fished in the traditional way, with oars or sails.

Windlass or Wink

Anchor with 100m Line

Crutch

Thole Pins

Culch Board

Dredge

Oars

A starfish or *cramp*, eating an oyster

Nowadays an oyster gauge is used to measure the shells. If an oyster passes through the ring, it is too small and must be thrown back to help preserve stocks.

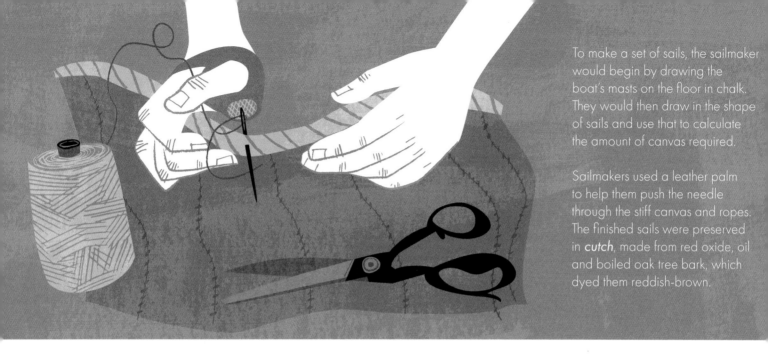

To make a set of sails, the sailmaker would begin by drawing the boat's masts on the floor in chalk. They would then draw in the shape of sails and use that to calculate the amount of canvas required.

Sailmakers used a leather palm to help them push the needle through the stiff canvas and ropes. The finished sails were preserved in *cutch*, made from red oxide, oil and boiled oak tree bark, which dyed them reddish-brown.

SAILMAKING, NET MAKING AND BOATBUILDING

For every fisherman working at sea there were several more jobs ashore. Almost all the fishermen's tools and equipment were made locally by skilled craftspeople and communities were much more self-sufficient than they are now.

Nets were made by hand, from hemp and other natural fibres. The old Cornish term for making nets was **breed** (from braid) and **beet** meant to mend them (from the Old English, betan).

Cornish boatbuilders were highly skilled at shaping the hulls for maximum speed. Speed was highly prized as the first boats to return got the highest price for their catch. In 1900, a new lugger with sails and fittings might cost around £200, around two thirds of which was the cost of the timber.

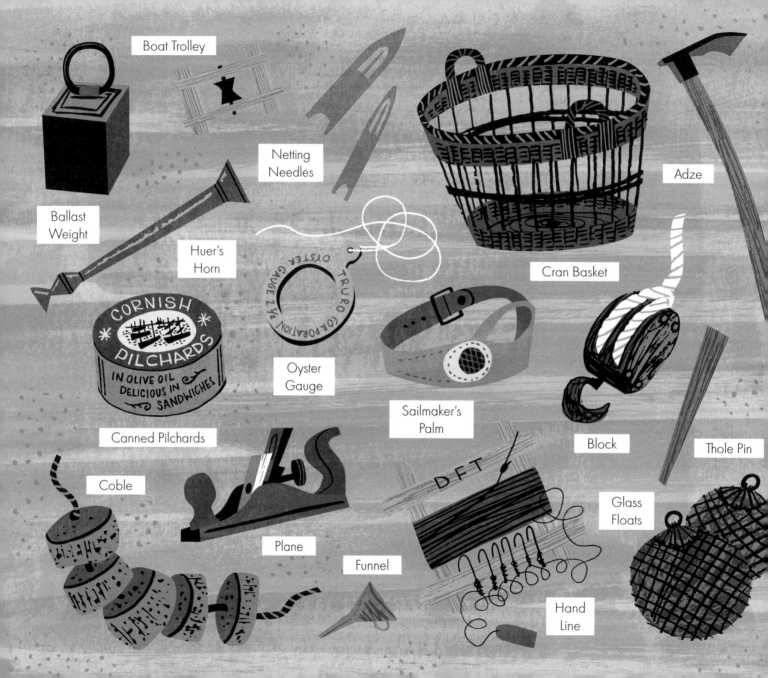

Boat Trolley

Netting Needles

Adze

Ballast Weight

Huer's Horn

Cran Basket

Oyster Gauge

CORNISH PILCHARDS
IN OLIVE OIL
DELICIOUS IN SANDWICHES

Canned Pilchards

Sailmaker's Palm

Block

Thole Pin

Coble

Plane

Funnel

Glass Floats

Hand Line

Cork Floats

Rowlock

Thigh-Length Boots

Traverse Board

Sou'wester Hat

Serving Board

Hand Capstan

Withy Pot

Oyster Dredge

Anchor

Longline Basket

Deck Lantern

Sailmaking Scissors

KNIT-FROCK

The gansey or *frock*, was a fisherman's jumper. It was usually navy and very tightly knitted, without seams, to help protect against the elements at sea.

Fishing families could rarely afford to buy clothing, so knitting was a necessity. Ganseys were often knitted by women for their husbands or sweethearts, but men frequently knitted too. Fishermen sometimes had a work gansey, and a more elaborately patterned one for Sunday best.

A gansey would take weeks to make and if it was navy, stain the knitter's fingers blue. Patterns were knitted from memory and customised to the wearer. For example the sleeves might stop short of the wrists, so they wouldn't get saturated or snagged as the fishermen worked, or the wearer's initials might be included in the design.

The garments were also endlessly repaired, remade and handed down, so unlike modern clothing, each one was totally unique.

This book is just a brief introduction to Cornish fishing heritage but there is much more to find out in the county's beautiful harbours and along its rugged coast, as well as from the many wonderful books on the subject.

———————

BIBLIOGRAPHY

Hevva! Cornish Fishing in the Days of Sail by Keith Harris

A Boatbuilder's Story by Percy Mitchell

A Glossary of Cornish Sea-Words by Robert Morton Nance

Evening Star, the Story of a Cornish Lugger by Ken Shearwood

Boats and Boatbuilding in West Cornwall by A.S. Oliver

The Fishermen of Port Isaac by Geoff Provis

Memories of the Cornish Fishing Industry by Sheila Bird

The History of the Falmouth Working Boats by Alun Davies

Fishing: The Coastal Tradition by Michael W. Marshall

Sailing Drifters by Edgar J. March

———————

See more work by Matt Johnson and buy prints at
mattillustration.uk

Special thanks to Kathryn and Joe.
Dedicated to my dad, Phil, who loved the sea.